salmonpoetry

*Celebrating 35 Years
of Literary Publishing*

Virtual Tides
PAUL CASEY

Published in 2016 by
Salmon Poetry
Cliffs of Moher, County Clare, Ireland
Website: www.salmonpoetry.com
Email: info@salmonpoetry.com

ISBN 978-1-910669-38-9

COVER ARTWORK: *Rosie O'Regan*
COVER DESIGN & TYPESETTING: *Siobhán Hutson*
Printed in Ireland by Sprint Print

*Salmon Poetry gratefully acknowledges the support of
The Arts Council / An Chomhairle Ealaoín*

"unreal things have a reality of their own"
Wallace Stevens

Acknowledgements

Poems in this collection have appeared in the following publications: *Brain of Forgetting, The Pickled Body, New Eyes on the Great Book, Colony, The Elysian, Levure Littéraire, North West Words, Shamrock Haiku Journal, Agamemnon Dead, New Planet Cabaret, The Penny Dreadful, The Stony Thursday Book, Fulcrum, Southword, The Irish Examiner, Crannóg* and *Live Encounters*.

My deep appreciation to Kobus Moolman for his generous and masterful commentary, and to poets Alan Titley, Hélène Cardona, Dairena Ní Chinnéide, Billy Ramsell and Thomas McCarthy for their cherished insights.

Thanks are greatly due to the Cork City Council Arts Office for a 2013 arts bursary, which helped to create much of the time needed to complete this body of work.

I am indebted, as ever, to Jessie Lendennie at Salmon Poetry for three bountiful week-long residencies above The Salmon Bookshop in Ennistymon, Co.Clare. I am also very grateful to Siobhán Hutson at Salmon, for her close attention and intuitive eye.

To Rosie O'Regan, for weaving this extraordinary cover from petals, leaves and love. Weave half the same of me I'll be a very wealthy man.

CONTENTS

Paper Stone Circles

stone turns to paper in her eye
as she filters cycles of light
into circles of paper stones

her eye is a stone circle
a near-infinity of light
that sees the circle as finite

the near-permanence of stone
the almost endless circle
is light, impermanent as paper

stone and white butterflies
circle and circle her
she questions their sentience

stone ancestors
paper-light circles
she sees them say

she hears their paper voices
say, know your own time
be light, circle, stone

Quiet Calf

Wring us out, stretch us taut upon the gray bone frame
Scrape us down lunellum-thin as the wide moon blade

For we are codex and caesar, the offspring of mechanical gods
Inflections pressed in virtual folios we are to each cow its calf

Carry the jasmines; the saffrons of our time, calcite prophecies
emblazoned in the cockled ranges, gilded in continental divides

Under a fallen pejeng moon white buffalo spirits pound to crush
the hard harmonics of history in us, down to a form of raw time

They amplify the faded velleities that cling to its valley walls
as *calligraphy* the word (and true consort of vellum) — elegant

to pen as *alfalfa* — is all flair and flourish in the nourished nib's
unending congress. In streams of ink-song, tear-strewn tendrils

fall from the gyre-eye drumhead skies, the bodhrans and banjos,
timpanis weave, interleave our celebrations, the flint of our lives

Bear too the wildfire children tapping céilís on the counterhoop
absorbed in the patience of elm, loose-bound for gatherings yet

to come. Flexed, each breath is an age of song deep-stitched
into wrinkled silence, where cockleshells pucker from under

ancient sand. Outroam the Runicus quiet one, deliver whole
these few sweet heartbeats, these glimpses of humanity

a small measure

stars are born, people die
more stars than people
by far reborn as stars

and more stars than grains of sand
the number of grains of sand?
(7.5×10^{18} grains of sand)

seven quintillion, five hundred
quadrillion grains we believe
(give or take a few grains of sand)

the number of stars, 70 thousand million,
million, million stars (the same number
as molecules in ten drops of water)

so there are more worlds
in eleven of your teardrops
than stars (or grains of sand)

Stone Circle Circle

soles on fire
spring from stone tip
to stone age stone tip
around the circles
of characters
distinct

Knockagilla
Grange Carriganimmy
Lissyvigeen Carrigagulla
Kenmare Knockraheen
Gurteen Reananaree
Dromroe Gortanimil
Uragh Carrigaphooca
Dromohilly as tribes Rosnacalp
Shronebirrane some tall, split Teergay
Cashelkeelty thin as a wisp Coolaclevane
Ardgroom or squat Currabeha
Derreentaggart the very shape of they Knockanierk
Derrynafinchin who lugged and Drombeg
Maughanaclea shoved Reanascreena
Cappanaboul Maulatanvally
Cullomane Carrigagrenane
Kealkil Bohonagh
Dunbeacon Lettergorman
Baurgorm Knocks
Cullenagh

and strewn stones
remnants of spells
to expel spirits
of mischevy, magpies
hop the periphery
no matter what shiny offering

For Pointing at the Sun

1.

Just as the pillars meet a mile above the architrave
A sky splinter plummets to puncture the floodplain

A standing stone of city glass acute enough to scrape
the skyline, raze the tideline, wield a fist of cumulous

A capstone of progress is washed clean by the sun
A stylite-engineer tests the lean of the cornerstone

As gravity, reversed in the top percentile sends
rich minds skyward, just clouds for parachutes

The man with the paraglider has built a ramp
at the very top above his penthouse eyrie, early

everyday spirals down around a thousand windows
a thousand silent lightboxes empty as lives en suite

There's sand from the rock of Barra in the concrete
from Ballingeary, Inniscarra, Atlantic in the glass

2.

River waters laugh into history's estuary
where floods ever migrate, recede to accede

The tower's north side is half-lost in cloud reflection
The sun burns a portal through the plexus of its illusion

Passing by traffic lights bus windows airbrush passengers'
faces with fresh graffiti, stone walls, posters, pedestrians

In a main street mirror, a blur catches its owner off guard
He sees the speed but not the face of his puzzled likeness

The stock room of the medi-clinic is filled with plastic
cards, booze-rattle, metal quakes from the ALDI aisles

From further back in the queue, the teller's eyes are colourless
At the till, only a hint of copper glints from the vanished blue

At the window end of the bar the afternoon runs like a film
    into the pint glass
How intimate the world turns through the distance of surfaces,
    how oblivious

3.

New lives shimmer up and down the soundproof aquarium
Imagine immortal interiors, the small releases from gravity

Street shoulders prefer the give of lime, of sandstone, the weights
of newspaper and lateral symmetries, urbanities, familiar rhythms

A splinter of sky has pierced the riverbed, recalibrated
the azimuth, realigned migrant magnetites and micro-

climates for swallows to clear, with token sundial shadows
arcing slowly over fates and *fulacht-fiadh* inspired jacuzzis

Designer stone circles distinct as sunken sculptures in Cancun
Reefs reset for Tartarus in nine short days, an artificial equinox

Corals of consequence, stark and lifeless in the seething seas
Artefacts of glass and stone whose only sculptor is silence

From the crest of Patrick's bridge, the Lee stirs life into city lights
A moon frogleaps across a seal's back into the neon subconscious

Stone Reflection

for Frank McNamara

The stones are many and large
consider where to set them down
sons and daughters, ancestors

two rings
one of petrified druids
one of petrified crones
huddle

their still, ancient conversation
trapped in a torus hum
for three thousand winters
vigil oscillates in the sea air

a field of gulls
a field of crows
a sheep circle
in the memory of lichen

we are strangers
from beyond the world's ocean
children rush underground
blue, brown, eyes of green

strain from the ringforts
the lists
from inside hills
boulders and oak

the druid stones,
the crone stones unfold
their roots wrestle free
and still we come

steady through the deepest slit
we slip
our silent eyes
our prophecies

in hundreds we ribbon
the length of the silver way

Boghole

for John W. Sexton

the slop migrant vortex of turf muck
near swallowed him whole one grey farm day

he said, but for a bubble of air
caught in his jacket and but

for the tight wrists of *Fionnán* the wiry,
oh purple god of moor-grass, he was a sure goner

not an ear within range, nor an echo
of those frantic syllables survived

one time, one near took a full horse
he said, but for a prehistoric farmer

vice-grip on the tailbone
as another held the head

the black mud swallowed four megalithics
then belched in final surrender

bogholes in the city are invisible
people just can't see

when you're up to your lower lip in one
eyes everywhere, and so few hands

International Citizen

The eyes are passports
as the eyes of wildcats bright beneath the moon
that say, *we are from here*

as oxygen water sun are
arctic tern, shearwater, sandpiper, godwit, wheatear
as monarch, the humpback are

the probing nostrils of newly acquainted
rhino, hundreds in the pitch black at lake rendezvous
from miles every which way

dawn leaves only footprints.
Ghosts in New York, Seoul, Damascus have mouths
that sound as birds or goats sound

Who drew these lines between us?
In the daylight, their busy heads control remote bodies
passport gazes set straight ahead

Tides

1

south of the equator
a hundred melon-headed whales
beached by sonar

click long codas out into the deep
we have become where we have been
have stood in the water

have seen the sea from the sky
when the only cloud
is the moon

we will remember you

2

we fall from sibilance
to susurrus, through echoless oceans
inflections colour, accents hue

do we forget the sea?
the rain?
the we that remains?

when the tide is out
the we there
forgets the sea

we betray ourselves again

3

arrive and all is home
leave and all is home
leave and arrive and all is home

the wind will not stop stealing our voice
our voice will not stop arriving home
to a country imagined

as are we, in these solstices
eclipsed
by the next imagining

the swallows have come early

Dandelion

A hundred florets and seeds
Bitter cream of dandelion soup
dent-de-lion salade sautée
Tooth of lion wine, few know

there's a good half calorie in the small flame
& twice the chance
for dissociative identity disorder to arise
in the Irish daisy root

for milk witch tears in the coffee
pee-a-bed, wet-a-bed
dog-piss in the pavement cracks
the mountain paths

Swine snout ruffles appetite
settles gut of truffle hog
heals injured human skin,
inflammation, relentless

weeds of viral antiobiotica
so-called 'saw-toothed, gangly-stalked'
puffballs – just bursting with
vitalities – *in refrains of A & C!*

But these faceclock encroachments
anti-oxidants ticking out the right pulses
for tonics and bloods, infections
the *wildest* of afflictions

they neutralise the pesticides we kill them with.
General Lion Tooth's root extract
is firing up the frontlines
of World War C –

'selectively targeting &
                        reminding cells
to commit suicide'.
Worm Rose. Butter Flower, Taraxacum.

A hundred florets
a hundred seeds and their feathery parachutes
just oozing with rubber-grade
latex laughter

Indoor Forest

If your urban life is leaf-free
one might say
you could bring the forest to you

to a wide south-facing sill
solar steeped and deepened
with a small table, enough

for sixty pint-sized pots
ten say, by six
with seed varieties endless

cheap as compost on e-bay
green up those phalanges
rein in the continents

with maple jacaranda coral
spruce acacia wattle and
after two careful winters

a forest
spread open, bough
to open bough

coral trees
losing hearts
all day long

drifting lotus root
breathing
the wet light

Inside the Bonsai

after Yehuda Amichai

You visit me inside the bonsai
together we can hear the secateurs
clipping around and around us precisely
You whisper to me

I trust your words
because they carry grains of salt
the way real seaweed
carries salt from the sea

I press your fingers to my lips
this too will shape the future
and your fingers are cool
the way a hot day is blue

these things are all true
You visit me inside the bonsai
and you'll wait with me here
until the secateurs complete their work

Last Wildflower

for Rosie

I scaled the cliffs of Moher
to write about the tourists
trekked south till there were no more
barriers, signs of stick men falling
to where I could breathe
alone

right up at the edge where I have always been afraid
                                of imagining
that I have always been
                        and forever will be   falling
    imagine
                    being afraid of *imagining*
                                                    falling
and let go
            spilled
                    back
                            eyes to sky
clutching burren blossoms   picked for you

I went in gannet-deep
shot straight into the air
to reclaim my still form
then danced
in the tower of Moher
above the clear blue day

Trace memories of this scene recur
mitochondrial microfilm coaxed open by the sun
these cliffs those islands, the fall
and lay of it, the width & breadth of it
the countless known unknowns
like Mog of the Hundred Battles

or why Clare isn't in Connacht.
But writing as I walk now
should this ledge crumble
please know you were
the last wildflower
on my mind

Question of Memory

when we won the five in a row I
played in goal just like my father
and grandfather before me and in
five years no sliothar passed me by

they made me goalie of the century
I had women coming out my ears
and houses bought and free pints for life
and the statue was a mighty touch

I'm still my favourite audience
The more I remember, the more
I start swelling with pride, with all
those great things I wish I'd done

Ultima Thule

Everything you can imagine is real
— Pablo Picasso

With each new button invention, fewer and fewer remember an actual world, where fellow beings navigate consciously, subconsciously through the somehow rhythm-regulated, fractal throng of Us. A lightning strike at the snooze button stretches the teats of reverie. Some press elevator buttons or traffic-light pedestrian buttons repeatedly, as if these woodpecker urgencies could inoculate them with spirit. With time invariably being an issue, navigating the city becomes an art. Frantic digits commit daydreamers to blinkard leaps out of doorways, into prams and old ladies. Into me. Stop me in a world of go-go-go, though I'm rarely stopped, thanks to a thousand days of street ballet in busy cities. But I stopped to realise that people had stopped realising. Smart glasses are on the way, like it or not. There's someone beeping at stopped traffic. The wake of a straddling jaywalker sets off a thousand domino queues of exponential chaos.

We're all artists of life. Of living. But artists *for* life? If Cork's taught me anything, it's that to create culture, you have to *cultivate* it. The president of the Intergalactic Federation of Light once told me that one can breathe their way towards anything. You'd wonder if the children of Spiritus: *inspiratio; inspirare; inspiracion* — are somehow in a recession of their own. That in all its invisible ubiquity, inspiration is in constant waiting for the right acoustic. State of mind, some say. Up to the muse. Down to 99% sweat. And like lightning loves a dry storm, with all the more chance for its fiery progeny to spread the original conception, immaculate infernos of inspiration rage against the teeming, taming rains, the chaos and tantrums of traumatised offspring take time, to take on the infinite drizzle of care, sizzle of patient creation geo-forming primordial miracles into Art. *Elusive promiscuity thou, from whence doth thou spring? Où vous cachez-vous?*

ici

Do you laze languidly in the slow steam of the gym sauna? Jubilate in the coals of *Timiti Kundam*, or wait submerged to jolt the ice-swimmers of Lapland? Some say you're sip-deep in a crisp pint of stout, laughing in the abyss of absinthe or placid in the clear plasma of *poitín*. A form *itself* of firewater. *Vin rouge* rarely warms the heart it is said, without glazing the soul with notion. So much for un-cultivating the drinking culture, I know. Forget the mystery of it, there's no maybe about it when all the cogs start spinning, eyes spiralling open as heartbeats samba their bass amplifiers up to the inner ear, the kindling of the belly ablaze with obsession. No mistaking it. Perhaps its nuclei spin at the core of all elements, and like electrons, occupy more than one space in time, waiting only for the right being-state to inhabit. Teasing us lucid servants of wonder at play and poised to carousel its will out into the insatiable world. It seems oxymoronic everytime I hear it, but we have for the most part forgotten to breathe. To *re-*inspire. Nirvana knows I'm no exception.

Surviving each unreachable itch, we live as if we'll live forever. Perhaps we lost some *a priori* wisdom when we screamt ourselves into this world, something drowned in those traumas, inquisitions of infancy. Why this great instinct for beauty? To bud a thing of beauty and watch it flower. Maybe it's a good thing we're all so preoccupied. I find things when I'm not looking for them, and don't when I am. Excruciating paradox. For most people, reading *poems is as rare as seeing fireflies or the lights of Ultima Thule.* You know they're out there, where to find them and how gorgeous they can be. You just can't be bothered. Everything's on youtube now.

So I purge the dark ink from this tomb of night with the squeeze of an eye, a squinting out of some inner light. With most of us out of our minds from fluoride and advertising, tsunamis of tech and bug-bytes of info, I'm most certainly *as mo mheabhair ar fad*. Desensitised at least in *some* sense. As many senses as dimensions, I'm out of it. And who isn't out of touch, out of care, out of time, in some sense? Perhaps it's not just darkness, but imagination that all this artificial light steals away. Dreams in exile, imagination too subdued, or bored. Once we're all blind to this world, surely it must cease to exist. All left is this vision, this hearing, this heartbeat. All else could vanish, as if magic were impossible, as if perception couldn't fuel the perceived, as if the unseen, the untouched, could not cease to be. Like memory. Like inspiration.

evolving the hypnic jerk

obsolescence is an ouroboro. its opalescent scales like goosebumps have long outlived their uses – like most bodily hair. try a fully-functional vemeronasal, olfactory organ for size and truly follow your nose, punch-drunk on pheromones. the male uterus, the male nipple, additional nipples in the female. scrolls of junk dna that once peddled vitamin c. the pinna muscles and darwin's point to aim the ear and pin-point sound. 'useless body parts', the near extinct plantaris, pyramidalis, subclavius, palmaris muscles, from when we fled on all fours and hung out in trees, safe and sound with the hypnic jerk. our third eyelid and cellulose-pestles, the wisdoms and appendix. the tail and neck rib. thirteenth rib. primitive reflexes like the Palmar Grasp, to name but a few in the physical human. now, losing touch may soon be declared impossible, 'getting lost' removed from the world database of practical phrases. personal boundaries live no longer than wi-fi wavelets. though nothing recent, individual memory is still endangered. what the android alone has sent packing for antiquity. physical memory along with the physical world. analog was once a god, the typewriter cherished, floppy disks and hard drives that analysts in silicon valley still bow to everyday. celluloid was a god. the disposable camera. the photo album a social occasion. the polaroid. modem and camcorder, video and record stores, players all but antique. cassettes extinct as the walkman, MiniDiscs and the soon to be, 'once mighty' DVD. e-history books that feature nostalgic essays on Atari, the Commodore 64, Windows 1.0 to 10. broadband competes with air to replace the GPS, CB and ham radio. talking, now as in decline as incandescent light bulbs. journals, comics, classifieds were once worthwhile. soon collective memory will not conjure the landline, answering machine, the facsimile. annual fortunes spent on diaries, the filofax, rolodex, alarm clock, the wristwatch, pager, calculator and leather tie. adieu to the signature, a gesture as personal as the lickable stamp, the pen-pal, the pen, the greeting card, postcard and the handwritten note. carbon paper, correction fluid, the satchel, the classroom, the post office. the office – all entering a new dark age. time chews, digests encyclopaedias, thesauruses, the dictionary and phonebook. the phone box. the family shop. the flea market. the humble cork. oil. certainty. identity. the actual. no need now for the movie extra, the film score orchestra, personal assistant or bricklayer. copper wire and paper were a thing, the shredder praised in poems. personal cheques, currencies, cash and credit card swipers. blind dates are simulated. tollbooth operators and personal care assistants consigned to fragments of figments of outsourced reminiscence. who will remember the car manual, the manual car window, the combustion engine, or the car key? soon tube tv and rabbit ear antennae will exist only in the v.r. museum archives. while etymology, is riddled with obsolescence, like the rest of the history family. as obsolete pilots marvel at the propeller and the piston, the travel agent becomes defunct. the catalogue. the foldable map, ordinance surveys. the face-to-face meeting. the insinuation. no-one misses long-distance charges or planned obsolescence. soon bookstores and cinemas. the website. the web. the cigarette. taste and tastebuds. language. natural seed, ninety percent of nature. the secret, the sacred, the paradox, the original anything. humanity's humanity in haptic decline, but for a hypnic jerk of the mind.

Virtual Companion

this android I married
this heart that is not a phone
this answer-any-question-in-the-world
machine

unquestioning, backup brain
ever-ready scrabble companion
sci-fi fantasy come true
and namer of stars

you're a legless, personal typist in longhand
media mogul
radio, mp3 player, home theatre
bank teller and one-stop shop

instant news
weather vane
compass rose
master-slave umbrella for cyber rain

pocket pc
instant handicam
voice-to-text poet pad
and digital grave

you morph to a mirror in a click
Some backgammon with that coffee love?
oh torch of blackest night
oh map-master, global positioning amigo

precision time machine
trusty teleporter
   dearest, life remote-control
   take me now

on second thoughts

It's time for that coffee and packing up of principles

and off to the imagined life, the lock of that stolen key

Could it be this torrent of barbarity we hear and see

keeps us in constant mistrust of our own humanity?

Being spoilt isn't just an expression, is it now?

We can only do a lot with a little for so long

and traffic is all about flow and avoiding pretzels

Nasturtiums in our mouths are worth gardens

for deserted nets won't capture lines, lives, nor

will reciting pi to a thousand places while high

as fifth century stylites, our monkey brothers

close at hand, Soon Mo Kong and Hanuman

finding Jupiter in the frosted pavements of the cities

There's so much more to what we've done than luck

Life won't run away at twenty-four frames per second

in its timeline of deadlines laid pipe-like in the depths

of an age when late winters meant hot summers, kudzu

colonising at a foot per day. So let's lay a full keel, flee livid with illusions of progress, the sky split by each in turn

for once shy and forever bitten, we wear all of our layers

we seek the unfound bodies that lie beneath the rain

shallow as a field of g.m. spuds in county Wicklow

and teach our phones to speak Irish so as to consider

the price of being 100% Irish-legal, the full cost analysis.

With the sacred now virtual, we're walking the world home

as we protest through spending saved and unsaved time

Why count the days in pairs of socks or human chains

and keys of corporate law and vagabondary?

A thousand years ago they'd all be dead men. What fools

take on the traits of film characters, splice fantasy to their

instinct? *You*, see beauty as a jungle of endless species

a menu unmeant to be written or told. Loss as an artist's

heart, a black goat, the angel's share calling the shots

and that's the kettle calling the hob more efficient for you

Though it may well be a case of mistaken identity crisis

we've nothing left to give but the desire to give

Let's take our souls down to the drycleaners for a spin

we've been stuffing the French press with ground-down

words, doomsday scenarios, temporary considerations

If you discriminate among colours you're a colourist

And those sixty-four twits who make the world go round

indulging in the odd few delusions of grandeur, singing

war as the appropriate response – and *then* of its nature

while others find teaspoons more lethal than knives

the lives of rolling stones won't end in their settling

What we imagine in dread can be actualised by all

the wrong people for we've imagined it, unrealised

Dark cumulous speeds along the edge of your iris

and in each, a flash – yes you too harbour lightning

We talk of the dreaded ends of those we love, wish

upon them more music, more life while we share

this one, dreaming in one tense, living the other

hoping beyond hope the inevitable turns evitable

Too much too soon too little too late too clichéd,

too unique, there's no true synonym for synonym

Now we're specialising in generalising in a time loop

of jumping through hoops, can't change how we feel

till we feel what we feel and the thing about avocados is

that downloading is our new favourite form of exercise

And how long is a moment? Excuse me a moment. I know

it's not time yet. Has your imagination too, been faithful?

A too cool fool, you say? Perhaps a too cool fool

but a happily too cool fool, in search of that silent L

in words where, the phone won't play dead for long

where the dead have been calling all day long

where summer thermals make earth-clouds of the trees

or, white-winged raindrops rise in pairs to the sky, only

to fall as caustic grains of sapphire sand, forget the house

in the hills, we should stay right here, clarity being such

a hard-won magnificence, and we so quick to cloud it

Diaspore

Some diasporas sustain massive, relentless lions of history.
Two of every five claim descent as their primary ethnicity.
Diasporas, in legal terms, habitually reside outside of a land.

This includes their children, citizens under law. It includes their grand-
children. Great-grandchildren only if the parent claims descent before the
question is born, a legal definition considerably small for any country.

Any bridge for foreign separation of tears is limited by status, leading
to a fluctuating, emotive definition. Persons in larger diaspora cherish
special ancestry. Live broad in its identity. The right terminates at the third

generation. This contrasts among countries. Causes see people flee all over
the world. How common flight is entirely correct. Emigration theory
could mean slow famine over years, as migrants consider the final straw

and other factors. People incriminate religion, rents and convictions
increase encumbered estates as well as existing rights. Agrarian crush.
Change quashed with death (champion for failed risings). Ceasing gold life.

fly agaric

in autumn, a sonnet of girls wash blueberries
for a mathematical picnic, solidity is
no concept, nor a blueberry pie
especially if well made
and in november

amanita illuminated hallucinated footprints
in you, where luck held no flame
tributes and habits forgotten
were great musics
muscaria

on horseback
music marries poetry
as do words ears. Real, loud
rebellious happenstance conjured by the djinns
of our daydreaming selves

matchbox

'You were lucky ... There were a hundred and fifty of us, living in a shoebox ...'

– Monty Python

I'd be a worthy multi-millionaire, not having to worry about all this clutter,
living in a tetris game built for faeries, where offering you coffee means shuffling

the plates over to the table corner, sink-dishes to the fridge-top,
(looking back we could all see ourselves as ice cream cones taken fresh

from the hands of the vendor on a day of mixed weather,
auspicious, but just a few minutes in your fingers are all sticky)

wash the plunger, fill the kettle from the lower twenty-litre
drum of fluoride-free *fioriusce* which, under the first, empty one,

waits undisturbed behind the chair on which the new book-
skyscraper has constructed itself, then shift the bookcase to reach

cups, unpack the tins to find the sugar, slide
the recycling from in front of the fridge for

milk, then one has to replace the sugar
to balance the shelf that holds the beans

on which the whole procedure rests. Coffee
beans. The grinder being always handy though

will not be an issue, however
the gas ring's hit and miss

given there's no more space
(second law of diminishing returns)

for bills to fit
through the flap, besides

having no matches
is the final

straw when
living in

a
matchbox

Bar Beings

Bar beings in some bars are unbearably bleak.
The bar-tops shine, beermats are all brand new
but there's a blast of bitterness, as broken beats
abound in the heavy, quiet bouts. Not that they're
always depressing bastards, I mean you wouldn't
hear them butchering the blues. I often just sense the
poor buggers just bursting to get buried into a bottle
of brandy or bacardi or bushmills. All those black-
labels, buds and becks just staring up at them like

lonely barstools, waiting to be boosted 'n birled on
some binge-benefit beach, way out of bounds. But they'd
blow the business, the burden, and the bank would
be bent on bouncing their bonds. Besides, they'd be
backstabbing the boss. So they bear it. I go from baffled
to bonkers just eyeballing them. What bowls me over
is seeing them brighten up a bit once the banter and
bustle begin. The busyness seems to abate the boredom
and bring a buzz. Banish the black bile.

Bar beings in other bars bear belonging well.
Even emptying bins you'll often hear them whistle
or hustle a bit of bebop maybe, a light breakbeat,
beatboxing their way along notabother, no matter
how back-breaking the barrels, they'd be belting out
Bowie or Bronski Beat, or the whole of Brewing up
with Billy Bragg. Or go ballistic with Black Sabbath.
Some barladies are ballerinas, pas de bourrée-ing their
bubbly bums and bellydancing up and down the boozer,

topping up bits 'n bobs in the liquid buffet while balancing
beers and bordeaux (basically blindfolded), beguiling
the last bead of baileys from the bottleneck as the buyers
flower like bindweed along the bar-counter. Bless them.
Happy to sort the breakages, with no brouhaha, ballyhoo

nor that quiet bitching that booms in the brain like a burst blood-vessel. Bomb, blare and barb-free bliss. Boundary-less breaths of fresh breezes. Bar beings that blaze bright as banshees burning bacchanalian bonfires – those highballs of beaming brilliance!

Water Signs

when I was young I used to love ambling out to the end of the high diving board and

```
                                                                swallow

                                                                diving

                                                                down

                                                                thru

                                                                the

                                                                one

                                                                ness
                                                                of
                                        , y                     g

above  air    water                loving          t                   r
          and
               the                    the                          a
               asmuchas          plunge                 i      v
   and I
     loved                    beneath

      thr

       u
       s
       t

         i

           n

             g

           t

             o
                                                                          r
                                                                          o
            the bottom          and hanging out          on  the   f l o
```

bit of craic

for Joshua

Slap Crack Thwack of the sliothar
of the perfectly connected golfball
where the b in ball is a one metal ping
like the T in t-shirt snapped into symmetry
(for de-wrinkling and folding, that is)

a pistol tries hard to compete
the way the air is cracked in war zones
over and over, missing the mark
and when was there not a war on somewhere
or the peck of a t-spoon on a hard-boiled egg?

The crack of a high branch in the Congo
cracks of the t-towel whipping wars in the kitchen
Clack of the post flap
of a thunderclap (when lit up) or just
the craic, snapple and top of the morning

to your drowsy, waking head

monkey's wedding

Hungry, we spied them in the trees before they fell
upon us, their tonguey claddings drunk on opposites,
her strewn trousseau of cloud the net that drew us up
from the muggy earth's hold as the king's minky wings
sang hot and low to the dangling jewels tingle-jangling
from her tresses, dazzling each token witness with no
duress but pure eye-bliss — then welcomed us to feast —

to ply us all with wonky monkey wedding wine (rain
and sunshine at the same time) were winged into middling
monks for a while, a minute, we winked and drank and
smoked from the old yoke of jungle dreading mind signs
made merry reason sound dangerous and pinky-swore

not to tell what we saw, still shocked as tourists in skis
woken midsummer without the snow, were told to go.

Itch

Do you too stretch out an itch you cannot scratch?
As chimps flout our kitch conventions, quench,
quash their flinching patches of ticks, lice, a tickle
waits for no chimp. No, there's no unreachable itch
no cherry-picking moments when no-one's watching
to line stitches under fingernails for extra friction
or the untimely irritation in the shoe, or those
no-go-zone concentation-killer clarity hijackers.

A female crouches in mosquito-ridden water reed
watches humans hitch her sisters to a thin wire
reaches for a scream she cannot pitch as we,
void the itch of time, scrape proof from view
till all its vetch, snatched up leaves but a wretch of
moments left to catch, to fletch our chinese signs
with cheers and cheery syllables. We want to chill.
Fetch up the chargrilled choices, try sauerkraut

and stout for breakfast, perhaps forget the itch.
Since school days, whence mitchers and snitchers
first sprang, sprouted, we pout from our comforts
hatch batches of soon-to-be-scrapped plans. Chink
glasses, stretch out the fictions we cannot scratch.

Laughing Lama

"Difficulty comes with the third mosquito"
— Dalai Lama

how shall we lift the blindness he asks
   between fits of laughter
that hides the imperceptible source of their joy?

when we could all be laughing
through the day, through loss,
death. Just imagine the world so

once-stoic, briefcase emissaries now laughing
chuckling bus drivers, beggars in stitches
prisoners in spasms, celebratory dustbinmen

judges. guinness book records
for the longest, loudest howl,
shriek and scream of laughter

most aesthetically pleasing giggle
most people laughing at once
deepest and highest pitches of hysterics

signs in operating theatres
No Laughing During Surgery Please
competitions for the sweetest

most experimental
immediate, quickest off the mark bursts of laughter
most infectious

trios and quartets of laughers
national orchestras of merrymaking
and International public laughing holidays

a ministry of mirth
it's so simple
he sees

takes a breath
and bursts
into laughter

Cure

for a Robyn

A friend of mine
revealed the secret

unlikely as a robin
to migrate each season

she arrives in spring
turns south to winter

then back for autumn
and away to summer

spring winter autumn summer
spring winter autumn summer

and younger
every year

Où avez-*vous* appris le Français ?

with thanks to Hélène Cardona

Je suis parti à la recherche de moi-même en France, oui
j'ai parcouru le pays
jusqu'à Grenoble
où j'ai demandé
à deux commerçants âgés

Êtes-vous des cigarettes ?

Ceci, après dix ans d'apprentissage
de la langue à l'école – J'en étais mortifié
après quoi, j'ai travaillé
avec deux frères
de Marseille

Fadi et Papi. *Merci!* Quelle vie incroyable!

Nous mangions seulement
des steaks pour le déjeuner
peignions toute la journée
dormions, rêvions, réveillés par
le miel de mots nouveaux

sur la langue

Living with Six Lovers

m'adores-tu, moi?
tu sais que je t'adore, toi.

liebst du mich?
du weisst ich liebe dich.

uthandani mina?
wazi ukuthi ngithanda wena.

ek's lief vir jou, ja my liefie, jy.
en ek wiet jy's lief vir my.

a stór, táim i ngrá le tusa.
cinnte, nach bhfuil tú i ngrá le mise?

and isn't it odd my sweet
how in english we no longer rhyme?

What the Frack

as we look forward
  to paying for more dumbing-down
of fluoride in the water charges

We can look back with fondness
  to a long proud age of free
transcendental medication

on tap

but between us, fear not
  despair not, for our fine future
is furnished with the highs

of a new fracking-laced legacy
  and we'll all have our money's worth
with that added dose of methane

free chemicals, unspellable
  and a mere spark-away
from a new water

that burns

Initial Pill

a date-activated oil spill response
following fire and subsea blowout
initiated a relief flotilla

of mechanical vessels to skim
supplies of aircraft spray
(and guard 1,000,000 feet of day's end)

forecasting offshore protection
of sensitive power effectively
Assembled world-class doubts

resolved to escape the effects
of area dispersants
and plans for their use

Defence Forces Seek Artists

Top officials are refusing to comment on speculation
that modern military training techniques and codes
of engagement, are undergoing a revolutionary shift

towards anti-war activity, one example rumoured
to be a highly innovative diffusion gesture, aimed
to disarm aggression through immediate exposure

to spontaneous music, practical jokes, rap and dance.
The trend may well be spreading, as reports continue
of platoons trading hardware for guitars, microphones,

portable amps and venue space to hold non-stop concerts
without borders, as major arms manufacturers wield placards
alongside scrap-metal merchants from the anti-art movements.

Meanwhile Queen Sirikit still manufactures new reefs, dumping
tanks, armoured cars into the sea. Fish numbers have swelled
significantly, diverse now beyond expectation despite draconian

defamation laws, her generals' newly formed *a capella*
barbershop quartets (and popular youtube channels) allegedly
feature her royal highness throwing in the crown jewels

having borrowed the Irish Defence Forces strategy
to melt down all lethal metal objects to form cymbals,
xylophones, drums and instrument strings, plans

to adopt the ever more popular slogan
Sort it Out with Art! Poets with relevant
translation skills urgently required within

Ó Bhéal at Cruising Speed

four hundred tons of jumbo
takes sixty minutes
fifty thousand pounds of fuel
and forty winks to slip
into the thin stream and curve
of cruising speed

where at thirty five thousand A S L
and five hundred miles per hour
it burns less fuel per person

than a small economy car
all that's left now
is to keep it up there

alfalfa in cursive

so that the nib stays on the page
in continuous curlicue from the
ear of the first a to the last a's tail
in one fluid symbol of neverending
conjoined curves, I say, I write, *alfalfa*

and so that I may jib and tack
through the gusting of language
without pause, muscles of the
hand flowing in obescience to
the electric infinity of soundshapes

I say and write

alfalfalfalfalfalfalfalfalfalfalfalfalfalfalfa

Jack's Orchestra

These days we get away with a little reverb and echo, sfx, but way back then in the very first talkies, there'd be twenty blackboard dusters to clack out irregular feet while twenty rashers sizzled on a kingsize griddle for the rain, in the tinsel section the crunching of cellophane was a blazing fire, as sheets of tin and iron wobbled back and forth for storms and drums were thumped and pounded as the duster clacking quickened to the coconut-shells and their flickety-flacking horseplay dodging umbrella ribs swishing samurai style as knives were plunged into balsa planks and a mallet pounded pumpkins into smithereens, mashed frozen lettuces as melons dropped from 20-foot plus onto concrete, where crushed walnuts and acorns and apples were bones, carrots and celery snapped and twisted, were necks, fruit boxes cracked up phone books thumped and fists plunged into three-pound steaks as bricks rubbed each other in circles, seven sets of teeth crunching mints into the mic as corn-starch scrunched in a leather pouch for snowsteps and slapping leather gloves – flapping wings of doves the creak of an old wicker chair the rusty hinge, the staple gun

a metal rake or the car door
stomps on piles of audio tape
in bowls of jelly, baths of rags
from gravel pits to marble slabs
from curtain ruffling to doorbells
and brass handles and bicycle bells
and whatever else was needed for the
bang, cackle, clack, clank, clap, clatter,
crack, crackle, crash, gnash, jangle, patter,
rattatat-tat, rattle, slam, splash, snap, stamp,
t-tap, twang, yap, zap, bray, neigh, wail, gale,
blare, tear, blast, bark, snarl, roar, snort, squawk,
beep, bleat, cheep, creak, peal, peep, scream, shriek,
squeal, wheeze, bellow, yelp, chime, whine, whir, clink,
fizz, hiss, jingle, kachink, ring, ripple, sizzle, squish, swish,
tick, tinkle, trill, twitter, whisper, tick-tock, dingdong, bong, drop,
gobble, knock, mod, pop, plop, throb, growl, howl, plough, pound, moan,
boom, hoot, mew, tattoo, toot, swoosh, buzz, cluck, clunk, drum, glug, grumble,
hum, plum, put-put, rumble, rustle, scrunch, sputter, splutter, thud, thump, thunder, gurgle,
murmur or purr, Mr. Foley had it out back for sure, for any full-feature show, and in real time too.

Note: Sounds taken and rearranged from the *Handbook of Noise Measurement* by Arnold P. G. Peterson

Dia an Cheoil

Trí fheadóg bhí ag m'athair
A mbéalóg glas, gorm is dearg
Gaotha binne a séideadh
Maidin, iarnóin is oíche

Gach feadóg díobh ar nós a gcuid
Slat flaidireachta, ag lascadh an aeir,
Is chuir a gcuid duán faoi bhriocht mé,
Agus ghéill me láithreach gan teip

Sracadh den uisce mé le draíocht
Is mé nach mór ag eitilt
Mar is é an ceol, an Dia is láidre,
Bhuel sea, í ndiaidh an ghrá

Ach go cinnte an Dia is iontaofa.
Slogadh anois me, a Dhia an Cheoil
Le do chuid slata daite draíochta
Múnlaigh mé led fhuaim

A Mhúinteoir uamhnaigh
go dtí go mbeidh na píosaí beaga den eagla
Imithe, is go dtagann ar ais an solas

In ainm na feadóige moire glaise
Is na feadóige moire goirme
Is na feadóige moire deirge

God of Music *(Dia an Cheoil)*

My father played three tin whistles
through lips of green, blue and red
sweet winds blew
morning, night and noon

each a flyfishing line
split the air
hooked each pitch deep
into the underbelly of surrender

to be whisked from water
into perfect flight.
So, music is the mightiest god
after love and surely

the most eternal
Swallow me whole god of music
spin-flick those fly-rods, the colours of magic
mould me in tones of unheard notes

again, dear and dreadful teacher
'till these tiny scales of fear fall
away with the first rays of light

In the name of the green flute
   and of the blue
     yes, and of the red flute too

kudzu

Barely perceptible, it began at the window
frames, padding its broad leaves like moss

across the non stop-motion, bonsai forest floor
light greening to peripheral mist, eyes

consumed by pc screen, oblivious. Weeks streak
by as the low susurrus, virus-rustle covers

radio, bookshelves, printer and bonsai
a gradual stanglehold on the whole supply.

As it reaches the lip of the cold coffee cup, it takes
a while to find I cannot pry myself from the desk.

I watch as the forest of undergrowth
constricts like rhododendron my calves, binds

all below waist to the floor. I'm stranded.
Android just out of reach, not upgraded

to the robotic, limbed version in time. Voice
activation windows have all passed by. Roots

have plunged into every digital and organic
crevice. This is my final squeeze of art.

Photograph by Andy Ferreira

PAUL CASEY's début collection is *home more or less* (Salmon Poetry, 2012). A chapbook of longer poems, *It's Not all Bad*, appeared from The Heaventree Press in 2009. He has published poems in journals and anthologies in Ireland, the US, China, Romania, South Africa and online. Aside from writing poetry he is a multimedia artist, teacher, events director, editor, occasional filmmaker and poet in residence each May for Carechoice, a group of elderly homes in county Cork. He also edits the annual *Unfinished Book of Poetry*, verse written by secondary school students in Cork city and runs multimedia and creative writing courses for adults at the Cork College of Commerce. He is the founder/director of the non-for-profit poetry organisation, Ó Bhéal.